The Garden and ... Book

ga

Quizzes aren't just a test of what you know and don't know, they're an enjoyable way to learn. There is a variety of quizzes, on a range of subjects covering gardening and the natural world. Work your way through the book and then check your answers at the end. Get over 70% correct and your greenfingers are not in question. 50% to 70% is a fair effort, below 50% better luck next time!

The quizzes are also ideal for garden club barbecues and allotment society gatherings or amongst a few friends in the garden on a summers night or in deep winter when gardeners can only dream of juicy tomatoes, sweet peas and sunflowers.

Plant Type Quiz

Name the plant using the varieties as tips.

1. Bonaventure, Inca Dambuster, Hillcrest Delight

2. Tutti Frutti, Fire Queen, Parade

3. Charlie's Angel, Lord Nelson, Flora Norton

4. Hidcot Blue, Munstead, Blue Ice

5. Pink Delight, Nanho Blue, Big Blue

6. Devon Cream, Doris, Moulin Rouge

7. Elizabeth, Debutante, Bijou

8. Peticoat Frills, Picotee, Prima Donna

9. Lady Boothby, Snowcap, Dollar Princess

10. Fanciful Sweetheart, Musica, DeZire

11. Frenzy, Jazzy Wheeler, Fancy Wheeler

12. Snow Cloth, Gold Dust, Clear Crystals Purple Shades

13. Frosted Flames, Madame Butterfly F1, La Bella F1

14. Duchess, Comet Summer Days, Super Chinensis

15. Jolly Joker, Blackjack, Frou Frou

16. Oriental, Dawn Chorus, Ladybird

17. Inca, Sahara, Sunspot

18. Goldie's Gold, Honeycomb, Orange Boy

19. Cardinal Climber, Caprice, Sunrise Serenade

20. Florenza, Sunbright, Sunbeam

Bird Quiz

1. What colour is a female blackbird?

2. What big problem do Warblers have to often put up with?

3. What exotic bird has become established in the South West London area?

4. Bewick is a type of what bird?

5. A Rook and a Crow. Which is generally gregarious and which is generally solitary?

6. Why should you not put out desiccated coconut for birds?

7. In recent years what bird of prey has been re-introduced on the Isle of Skye?

8. What bird has a reputation for taking ornamental fish from garden ponds?

9. What colour is the head of a black headed gull in winter?

10. What garden bird is partial to nesting in old pots or kettles and is highly territorial?

11. Which bird is smallest, a Goldcrest, Treecreeper or Great Tit?

12. Thistles are a favourite food source for what bird?

13. How can you tell if a Great Spotted Woodpecker is male or female by looking at its plumage?

14. Pied and Grey are both what?

15. Which is the traditional summer visitor to the British Isles, Fieldfare, Redwing or Chiff Chaff?

16. Is a Kingfisher bigger or smaller than a Starling?

17. Which summer bird does not have a white underbelly, Swallow, House Martin or Swift?

18. Does a Dunnock prefer to feed on the ground or on bird tables?

19. What Owl due to an increase in breeding pairs resident in Britain does the World Owl Trust believe should be added to the British Orinithologists Union list of official British birds?

20. Why was the Great Crested Glebe nearly hunted to extinction in the 19th century?
a. Ate young trout b. head plumes used for hats c. meat was considered a delicacy d. male feathers used for flys by fly fishing anglers

21. What is the average life expectancy of a Blue Tit? a. 1.5 years b. 3 years c. 5 years d. 8.5 years

22. Blue Tit, Starling and Collared Dove. Which is the odd one out and why?

23. Western Capercaillie is a member of what bird family?

24. What region of the UK can the Western Capercaillie bird be uniquely found?

25. What is the average wing span of a Golden Eagle?
a. 3ft b. 4ft c. 5ft d. 7ft

General Quiz 1

1. Which is not a butterfly?
a. Cabbage White b. Pink Petal c. Red Admiral

2. What was the first name of the famous Blue Peter gardener Mr...... Thrower

3. What is the name of the conifer that became well known for creating garden border disputes amongst neighbours?

4. Haltwhistle in Northumberland claims to be what?

5. Which plant beginning with 'b' is brillant for attracting butterflies?

6. Ladybirds are good for controlling what pest?

7. The Optimum Population Trust, a leading group of demographers have declared what population to be the number that that the natural resources of the British Isles can sustainably cope with?

8. Jude the Obscure is a type of what?

9. Which seabird is sometimes called a 'Sea Parrot' ?

10. Which charity are against sewage? .... Against Sewage

11.Which popular garden plant was used by the Romans in their baths to scent the water?

12. Which country is associated with Koi Fish popular in garden ponds throughout the world?

13. Chile is the original home for which dramatic tree often found in stately homes and mature larger gardens?

14. Ermine is an alternative name for which British mammal?

15. Goldfinches, Magpies and Greenfinches all have something in common, apart from being birds of course. What do they have in common?

16. Edmund Hilary trained on which British mountain in preparation for his ascent up Mount Everest?

17. A Franciscan monk named a popular garden plant after

Leonhart Fuchs, a 15th century German doctor and herbalist. What plant was it?

18. What benefit is there to growing ferns in the UK?

19. Something in the garden became popular in the Netherlands during the 17th century, as a symbol for the House of Orange and independence, what was it?

20. How many tonnes of charcoal are estimated to be used in the UK every year for barbecues, that are not from sustainable sources?
a. None it is illegal   b. 10,000 tonnes c. 40,000 tonnes d. 80,000 tonnes

National Park Quiz

1. Peak District National park, Lake District National Park. Which is the largest?

2. In which state in America is Shenandoah National Park situated?

3. The Namib national Park in Namibia, Africa is renowned for what type of landscape feature?

4. Which national park in the UK has the Cheviot hills within it?

5. Which national park is located in Hampshire?

6. Which national park in the USA is the hottest and driest of them all?

7. Scotland has two national parks, Cairngorms National Park and Loch Lomond & The Trossachs National Park. Which is the furthest north?

8. The Mourne Mountains is a proposed national park in Northern Ireland. What bird was last seen in this area in 1836?

9. Crib Goch in Snowdonia National Park holds the record for what?

10. What animal is the symbol of Dartmoor National Park?

11. The Yorkshire Dales National Park is one of two national parks in Yorkshire. Dale originates from Nordic/Germanic what does it mean?

12. The rivers Tame, Goyt and Derwent flow through which national park?

13. The national park in Pembrokeshire, Wales was designated as a national park in 1952. What made it different to the others?

14. Which national park was first proposed as a national park in the original national park creation plans of 1947 , but only became a national park in March 2010.

15. The Brecon Beacons national park is made up mostly of what type of habitat?

16. How many people live within North York Moors National park? 250, 2,500, or 25,000?

17. The Broads, has how many miles of navigable waterways? 125, 250 or 72?

18. What type of deer has a stronghold in Exmoor National Park, Red, Fallow or Roe?

19. What world heritage site can be found in Northumberland National Park?

20. Loch Garten in the Cairgorms National Park is a regular

nesting site for what type of bird of prey?

General Quiz 2

1. Name the evergreen hedge that has created many a neighbourly dispute?

2. The Monkey Puzzle tree originates from which country?

3. What herb is regularly mentioned along with Rosemary?

4. The RHS holds a flower show at Tatton Park, which is in what County?

5. Name the popular type of goldfish found in ornamental garden ponds.

6. What plant is used in the treatment of Leukemia?

7. Soil can be Acidic, Alkaline or......?

8. Is a blue tulip fact or fiction?

9. What can be placed over Rhubarb to make it longer and more delicate?

10. What colour rose is associated with Lancashire?

11. What yellow flowering tree is poisonous?

12. What is the name for sculpting hedges?

13. What bulb plant could be described as having a facial hair problem?

14. Butterflies - Red Admiral, ... White?

15. Name the organic gardener with flower in his name?

16. What special attribute makes Lavender ideal for dry conditions?

17. What county did Capability Brown, the famous

landscape designer originate from?

18. I am a woody stemmed plant, usually branched near the base and lacking a single trunk....what am I?

19. What is a whip?

20. A Hybrid Tea is a type of what plant?

21. Where do Pelargoniums originate from?

22. What type of plants can be found in a rock garden?

23. Rhizomes are a type of what plant?

24. What herb beginning with 'A' has soothing properties?

25. A dibber is useful for what?

26. Cacti are often refered to as what?

27. Kale, Cauliflowers, Brussel Sprouts are all what type of vegetable?

28. A beer trap can help control what type of pest?

29. A cloche can help protect plants from what?

30. Shepherds Purse is a type of what?

The Grow Your Own Quiz

1. Moneymaker is a type of what?

2. What 'N' makes a good companion plant in the veg garden to act as a decoy and attract pests away from vegetable plants?

3. What plant is a well known natural fertiliser and can be grown to make a rich liquid feed?

4. The Honeyberry is a climbing fruit similar to blueberries. It is resistant to harsh weather. What region is it native?

5. Shirley, Poppet and Charlotte, which is the potato, which is

the pea and which is the tomato? (1 point for all 3 correct)

6. 'Salad Bowl' is a type of lettuce. Is it a hearting or non-hearting variety?

7. What rhubarb type vegetable is known for its decorative leaves and can be planted amongst flowers in borders?

8. Kale, Cabbage, Pak Choi and Broccoli can all be can be classified as what type of vegetable?

9. Carrots, Garlic and Radishes all have something in common, what?

10. What colour is the flower on Bush Marrows?

11. If Rhubarb is 'forced' what is the result?

12. If a fruit tree is trained along horizontal lines, what is this known as?

13. Why should Quinces be stored seperately from other fruits?

14. Black Mulberry bushes can reach a height of, 2-3 metres, 3-6

metres or 6-10 metres?

15. What were Kiwi fruits originally known as?

16. What is tip layering?

17. Dutch, Onion and Draw are types of what?

18. What is the watering can attachment on the spout known as?

19. For plants that resent root disturbance when being planted out what is suggested?

20. Cloches will protect plants from what?

21. Is mushroom compost alkaline or acidic?

22. French marigolds can be planted in the veg garden to attract what type of insect that will feed on aphids?

23. An inverted flower pot filled with dried grass and placed over a cane will attract what type of insect away from plants?

24. Name the veg garden enemy. Hedgehog, Garden Spider, Centipede, Millipede

25. What is inter cropping?

Tree Anagrams

Unravel the tree types

1. EVRHRILCIBS

2. PGNIWIEWOELWL

3. NBMLAUUR

4. NJEEMLAEPASPA

5. KOZEULMKNZEP

6. YRMLEBSORHSOC

7. BRAPLPCEA

8. PYCAUELSUT

9. TSCNESIOP

10. NDLOWEGYE

11. CUSAMLAPNH

12. EYSMACRO

Lakes & Rivers

1. What is the next major river south of the River Wear?

2. Two national parks have rivers in their names. What are the rivers? 1 point each.

3. What is the name of the largest natural lake in Wales?

4. Which of the following lakes is not in the Lake District?
a. Derwent Water b. Bassenthwaite Lake c. Hayeswater d.
Semerwater

5. Which reservoir in the UK holds the biggest volume of water?

6. When was the Serpentine lake in Hyde Park, London
constructed? a. 1580 b. 1730. c. 1884 d. 1926

7. Which county is home to the source of the Thames?

8. Put the following British rivers in order, longest to shortest. 1
point for all correct. Thames, Clyde, Severn, Avon

9. Does Birmingham have more miles of canals than Venice?

10. Name the Scottish Loch that holds more freshwater than all
the lakes in England and Wales combined?

General Quiz 3

1. Japanese Maples are renowned for what?

2. Which of the following is not a storage organ? a. Tubers b.
Rhizomes c. corms d. Nodals

3. What effect can bottom heat have on seeds?

4. Plum and Cherry trees can be prone to what type of fungus?

5. Before true leaves show on a plant, seed leaves appear. What are these first leaves known as?

6. How can you avoid scorching plant leaves?

7. The anther and filament make up what part of a flower?

8.which of the following type of potato is most resistant to common potato scab? a. Maris Piper b. Desiree c. King Edward

9. Heaps of soil on lawns can be a sign of what?

10. What makes leaves green?

11.Which is bigger, a Red Squirrel or a Grey Squirrel and where do Grey Squirrels originate from? 1 point for both correct.

12. Which county in Northern Ireland is home to the amazing coastal rock formation, the Giants Causeway?

13. Oxygen is a bi product of what natural process that occurs in plants?

14. What plant from the vegetable garden is good to grow alongside roses as it acts as a deterrent for greenfly?

15. Willows are home to how many species of insect? a. 20 b. 68 c. 250 d. 500

16. Sunflowers, Cornflowers and Yarrow are good plants to grow near your vegetable patch, why?

17. Which one of the following will not thrive in sandy soils?   a. bedding plants b. bulbs c. ferns d. carrots

18. Leaving a clump of nettles in your wildlife garden is advised, why?

19. Beer and frogs are not popular with what garden menace?

20. What plant beginning with 'S' is used for green roofing?

British Wildlife Quiz

1. What is the name for a female fox?

2. Great Britain has three native snakes, only one is venomous, which one? a. Grass Snake b. Smooth Snake c. Adder

3. Which deer is the largest? a. Roe . Red c. Fallow

4. What river mammal was introduced in Scotland on a trial basis a few years ago?

5. What mammal became extinct in England during the reign of King Henry V11 (1485-1509)?

6. What is a Leveret?

7. Are Badgers, a. Herbivores b. Omnivores c. Carnivores?

8. What is the estimated population of Otters in the UK? a. 600 b. 2,000 c. 8,000 d. 20,000

9. The Dangerous Animals Act of 1976 is thought to be one of the explanations for what?

10. Pre 1960 there was an estimated Water Vole population of 8 million in Britain. The most recent estimate in 2004 was just 220,000. Reasons for the dramatic slump in population has been put down to unsympathetic farming, loss of river habitat and being prey for what invasive mammal?

11. Chillingham Wild Cattle are thought to be the only survivors of wild herds that roamed the ancient forests of Britain. Since the 13th Century they have been kept at the same 365 acre enclosure in Northumberland. As of 2010, the size of the herd was a. 90 b. 254 c. 605 d. 832

12. What is a drey?

13. The Common Lizard, a lizard native to Britain is also known as the Viviparous Lizard. Viviparous refers to what? a. The ability to change colour. b. Mostly lives above ground in trees. c. Unlike most types of lizard they give birth to live young rather than lay eggs.

14. What mammal gives birth at sites known as rookeries?

15. Killer Whales (Orcas) swim in British waters. True or false?

16. For 1 point get both correct. A Stoat and Weasel are very similar, but one can turn almost completely white in winter, which one? Of the two mammals one lives quite a few more years on average than the other, which one?

17. Does a Hedgehog have a tail?

18. Which of the following statements about Natterjack Toads is NOT true. a. Their habitat is sand dunes b. They are good swimmers c. They can't leap very far d. They have a yellow stripe that can distinguish them from Common Toads.

19. Azure Hawker, Golden Ringed and Ruddy Darter are all types of what?

20. About 3,000 New Forest Ponies roam the forests and heaths of the New Forest in Hampshire, but who owns them? a. No one they are wild. b. HM the Queen c. The Government d. Commoners with grazing rights.

Herb Pairs

Match the herbs with what they are most associated with.

lamb, fish, cheese, potatoes, tomato pasta dishes, pot pourri, salad, oriental dishes, herbal tea, middle eastern dishes

1. Cumin

2. Chamomile

3. Rosemary

4. Parsley

5. Basil

6. Lavender

7. Chives

8. Sorrel

9. Ginger

10. Mint

General Quiz 4

1. Oak trees are home to an average of how many species of insect?
a.25 b. 100 c. 200 d. 300

2. Peacock and Painted Lady are types of what?

3. What is the correct term for a flower stalk, pedicel or filament?

4. Why should Willows be planted well away from houses?

5. Hairy Bittercress, Groundsel, Horsetail. Two are annual weeds, which is the perennial weed?

6. What type of soil retains water best? a. Clay b. Sandy c. Chalk

7. Does frost gather most in the lowest or highest part of the garden?

8. A carnivorous house plant has a planet in its name, what planet?

9. A bird has been re-introduced to Britain in recent years. The second part of its name is Bustard, what is the first?

10. If a Hydranger has blue flowers what does this indicate?

11. If a Rose has large flowers with one to each stem, what type could it be described as?

12. Impatiens is another name for which popular bedding plant?

13. Which garden herb is known for aiding digestion?

14. What benefit is there to setting up windbreaks and laying mulches in the garden?

15. Lavender, Rock Rose and Rosemary are tolerant of what?

16. French Marigolds can repel what pest from Tomato plants?

17. Why is straw often used as a mulch around Strawberries?

18. If plants are not potted on to bigger pots the roots begin to spiral and start suffocating the plant. What is this problem known as?

19. The Three Peaks Challenge is a popular charity fundraising activity that involves participants climbing three British mountains all within 24 hours. Ben Nevis in Scotland, Scafell Pike in England and Mount Snowdon (Yr Wyddfa) in Wales. For 1 point for both correct, which is the highest and which is the lowest of the three?

20. What tragedy befell the beautiful gardens of Heligan in Cornwall that led to their demise?

Environment & Greener Living Quiz

1. What was banned from aerosols to protect the ozone layer?

2. Name two types of renewable energy that use water? 1 point for both correct.

3. What did Trevor bayliss invent?

4. Fifty years ago the Aral Sea in Central Asia was the fourth biggest inland lake in the world. Due to mismanagement and excessive irrigation, how much has the lake shrunk by in recent decades? a. 20% b. 34% c. 49% d. 70%

5. What gas is produced if organic waste such as vegetable scraps are buried in land fill sites?

6. In 2007 how many tonnes of paper were recycled in the UK? a. 1,000 tonnes b. 3.3 million tonnes c. 8.6 million tonnes d. 20 million tonnes

7. Boneshakers were an early type of bicycle, invented in 1839. What advancement had been made from earlier models?

8. What percentage of the worlds bird species live in the Amazon rainforest? a. 10% b. 25% c. 33% d. 63%

General Quiz 5

1. What do peas use to cling to supports?

2. How should leeks be stored over winter?

3. Medlars are a type of what?

4. Jostaberries are a hybrid of what two well known fruits?

5. What type of timber is often used for greenhouses?

6. Alpine strawberries have an advantage over most other varieties of strawberry. What is it?

7. Which of the following facts about Asparagus is not true?   a. They are perennial b. They do not freeze well for storage c. They can be attacked by Asparagus beetles d. Asparagus has fern like foliage.

8. What is put in a drill?

9. Spiking, slitting and hollow tining are all methods of what?

10. Blanketweed will reduce what in ponds?

11. An arboretum is a collection of what?

12. What are lattice pots used for?

13. Snowdrops are often sold 'in the green'. What does this mean?

14. Ivy has aerial roots, this allows them to do what?

15. What can be done to protect hedging from damage from heavy snowfall?

Christmas Quiz

1. What country do Amaryllis bulbs originate from?

2. What Christmas decoration might you find growing in an apple tree?

3. The British Isles has one herd of Reindeer. Where can they be found?

4. Traditionally white Chess pieces are made from the wood from which type of tree?

5. Each year Bergen sends a Christmas tree to the people of Newcastle and the people of Oslo send a Christmas tree to London, in thanks for what?

6. What are Poinsettia flowers said to resemble?

7. What C can be added to Oranges to make a pleasant smelling Christmas decoration?

8. The tradition of burning a Yule Log, stretches back to when Pagans celebrated the Winter Solstice. In England, the log would usually be Oak, what type of log is traditionally used in Scotland?

9. For the UK to have an official White Christmas, according to the Met Office how much snow has to fall?

10. Prince Albert, Queen Victoria's German husband made the tradition of having a Christmas tree indoors popular. In 1841 he put a tree up in which royal residence?

11. Christmas Bush is a plant with small green leaves and cream coloured flowers, that turn a deep red in the run up to Christmas. In which country is it often used as a decoration?

12. Norfolk Bronze is a type of what?

13. The Sandringham Estate, where the Queen spends Christmas, has a 20,000 acre estate. What product is it most famous for producing?

14. How many Christmas Cards were recycled by the Woodland Trust scheme in January 2008, was it;
a. 12.8 million

b. 34.7 million

c. 49.3 million

d. 73.6 million

15. According to the RSPB, the Robin is resident in the British Isles all year round, and does not migrate. Which summer migrant might pass for a Robin if it was to paint it's chest red? It is slightly larger, hides out in thickets and sings a good tune.

16. Which type of Palm tree found in the Middle East produces a fruit often ate over the Christmas period?

17. Norway Spruce , Fraser Fir, Nordmann Fir, and Scots Pine are all sold as Christmas Trees. Which type is the most popular in the UK.

18. What type of bedding plant has a winter version that can survive the cold months?

19. What is placed in front of the Temperate Glasshouse at Kew Gardens over Christmas?

20. Bedford Fillbasket, Cromwell and Wellington are all types of what?

ANSWERS

Plant Type Quiz

1. Dahlias
2. Geraniums
3. Sweet Peas
4. Lavenders
5. Buddleja
6. Dianthus (Garden Pinks)
7. Clematis
8. Begonias
9. Fuchsias
10. Impatiens (Busy Lizzies)
11. Gaillardia
12. Alyssum
13. Antirrhinum
14. Asters
15. Pansies
16. Poppies
17. African Marigolds
18. French Marigolds
19. Morning Glory
20. Sunflowers

Bird Quiz

1. Brown
2. Getting a cuckoo in its nest.
3. Parakeet
4. Swan
5. Rooks are gregarious whereas crows tend to be solitary.
6. It can swell up inside their stomachs.

7. Sea Eagle

8. Heron

9. White

10. Robin

Multiple Choice

11. Goldcrest at approx 9cm is smallest. Treecreeper 12.5cm, Great Tit 14cm

12. Goldfinch

13. A male has red on the back of its head.

14. Wagtails

15. Chiff Chaff

16. Smaller

17. Swift

18. On the ground.

19. Eurasian Eagle Owl (Eagle Owl will do for a point)

20. b. Their head plumes were used to decorate hats.

21. a. 1.5 years

22. The Starling. The Blue Tit and Collared Dove are both non migratory birds, whereas the Staling does migrate.

Latin Test

23. Grouse

24. Scottish Highlands

25. d. 7ft

General Quiz 1

1. Pink Petal is not a butterfly.

2. Percy

3. Leylandi

4. The central point of the British Isles, measured from north, south, east and west.

5. Buddleia

6. Greenfly Aphids

7. 30 million or less
8. Rose
9. Puffin
10. Surfers
11. Lavender
12. Japan
13. Monkey Puzzle Tree
14. Stoat
15. Their populations have been increasing in recent years.
16. Mount Snowdon
17. Fuchsia
18. There is no major pests or diseases that affect them in the UK.
19. The Carrot
20. 40,000 tonnes

National Park Quiz

1. Lake District National Park
2. Virginia
3. Huge orange sand dunes
4. Northumberland National Park
5. New Forest National Park
6. Death Valley National Park
7. The Cairngorms
8. The Golden Eagle
9. Wettest place in the UK. Average rainfall of 176.1 inches per year.
10. Dartmoor Pony
11. Valley
12. Peak District National Park
13. It was designated for its spectacular coastline
14. South Downs

15. Moorland
16. 25,000
17. 125
18. Red Deer
19. Hadrians Wall
20. Ospreys

General Quiz 2
1. Leylandi
2. Chile
3. Thyme
4. Cheshire
5. Koi
6. Vinca, a strain of the Perrywinkle
7. Neutral
8. Fiction
9. A Rhubarb Forcer
10. Red
11. Laburnum
12. Topiary
13. The Bearded Iris
14. Cabbage
15. Bob Flowerdew
16. Small leaves
17. Northumberland
18. A shrub
19. A young seedling or grafted tree without branches.
20. Rose
21. South Africa
22. Alpines
23. Bulbous
24. Aloe Vera

25. Planting seeds
26. Succulents
27. Western Brassicas
28. Slugs and snails
29. Frost
30. Weed

Grow Your Own Quiz

1. Tomato
2. Nasturtium
3. Comfrey
4. Siberia
5. Non hearting
7. Swiss Chard
8. Brassicas
9. All have very low Nitrogen fertilizer requirements
10. Yellow
11. By 'forcing' the rhubarb by excluding light the plant will produce smaller, tender, pink stems.
12. Espalier
13. They have a strong aroma, which can contaminate the taste of other fruits
14. 6-10 metres
15. Chinese Gooseberries
16. Placing young stems from plants like the blackberry into the ground still attached to the parent plant. At the end of the season when the stem has grown roots it is cut away from the plant and a new young plant has been created that can be potted up and transplanted the following spring.
17. Garden Hoe Tools
18. Rose
19. Grow the seeds in biodegradable pots made from organic

matter that can be planted with the plant into the ground. They will protect the young roots and as they grow they break through the decaying pot..

20. Snow/frost/ice

21. Alkaline, it can be used to reduce acidity of the soil

22. Hoverflies

23. Earwigs, the pot can then be removed from the garden.

24. Millipede

25. Growing slow growing and fast growing plants alongside each other to make good use of space eg. Sweetcorn and lettuce

Tree Anagrams

1. Silver Birch
2. Weeping Willow
3. Laburnum
4. Japanese Maple
5. Monkey Puzzle
6. Cherry Blossom
7. Crab Apple
8. Eucalyptus
9. Scots Pine
10. Golden Yew
11. Chusan Palm
12. Sycamore

Lakes & Rivers

1. River Tees
2. River Dart (Dartmoor National Park) River Exe (Exmoor National Park)
3. Lyn Tegid (Bala Lake) 1,196 acres / 4.84km2
4. d. Semerwater. It is in North Yorkshire

5. Kielder Water in Northumberland. 200 billion litres.
6. b. 1730
7. Thames Head in Gloucestershire
8. Severn, Thames, Clyde, Avon
9. Yes 35 miles compared to 26 miles of canals in Venice.
However, Venice as a city is much smaller.
10. Loch Ness

General Quiz 3

1. Stunning coloured leaves in Autumn
2. d. Nodals
3. It can make seeds germinate quicker. Bottom heat is warming of the soil from below using heaters.
4. Silver Leaf
5. Cotyledons
6. Avoid watering during hot, sunny weather and water in the evening.
7. The Stamen
8. c. King Edward
9. Moles
10. Chlorophyll
11. Grey Squirrel. It originates from North America.
12. County Antrim
13. Photosynthesis
14. Garlic
15. c. 250
16. They all attract predator species of insects such as Hoverflies and Ladybirds that will feast on vegetable garden pests, like Aphids.
17. Bedding plants, as they have shallow roots. The rest all have deeper roots.
18. Butterflies lay eggs on them.

19. Slugs
20. Sedum

British Wildlife Quiz

1. Vixen
2. c. Adder
3. Red Deer. On average 175-230 cm / 5ft 9 in-7ft 5 in long
4. European Beaver. They were hunted to extinction in the 16th century due to the demand for their fur. A trial re-introduction is taking place in Argyll.
5. Wolves. The wolf survived until 1680 in the Highlands of Scotland according to official records, although it is possible based on a local legend the last wolf was killed in 1743 in Morayshire, by an elderly resident named McQueen.
6. A Hare under the age of one year old.
7. Badgers are omnivores, they eat both meat and vegetation.
8. c. 8,000
9. Big cat sightings in the countryside. When the act came into law it became illegal to keep animals such as Pumas. Rather than have them put down or taken, some owners are believed to have let them loose into the wild.
10. American Mink. They were brought over for fur farms in the 1920's, over the years some possibly escaped and others were released by anti fur farming protesters.
11. a. 90
12. A squirrels nest.
13. c. Unlike most types of lizard they give birth to live young rather than lay eggs
14. Seals
15. True
16. Stoat & Stoat
17. Yes, a small one.

18. b. They are good swimmers. They are not and can drown in deep water.

19. Dragonfly

20. d. Commoners. The term dates back to 1079 when William the Conqueror created the forest. It allows local people to graze ponies on open land in return for abiding by the forest rules. Todays commoners are people who own or rent land with common rights attached.

Herb Pairs

1. Cumin - middle east dishes
2. Chamomile - herbal tea
3. Rosemary - lamb
4. Parsley - fish
5. Basil - tomato based pasta dishes
6. Lavender - pot pourri
7. Chives - cheese
8. Sorrel - salad
9. Ginger - oriental dishes
10. Mint - potatoes

General Quiz 4
1. d.300
2. Butterfly
3. Pedicel
4. Roots can damage foundations
5. Horsetail
6. Clay
7. Lowest, cold air sinks.
8. Venus
9. Great
10. The soil is Alkaline/Limey

11. Hybrid Tea
12. Busy Lizzie
13. Peppermint
14. Protects soil against wind erosion
15. Dry weather
16. White Fly
17. To prevent Grey Mould, a fungal disease, from transferring from the soil to the fruits.
18. Pot bound
19. The highest is Ben Nevis, 1,344 m / 4,409ft, the lowest is Scafell Pike at 978m / 3,209ft. Mount Snowdon (Yr Wyddfa) is 2nd highest at 1,085m / 3,560ft
20. Before World War One the garden was maintained by 22 gardeners, 16 of them were killed in the war. The gardens fell into a state of disrepair for many decades before a full restoration began in the 1990s.

Environment & Greener Living Quiz

1. CFCs
2. Hydro electric power and wave power.
3. Wind up power crank radios and torches that require no disposable batteries.
4. d. 70%
5. Methane, when organic waste decomposes in compost bins above ground Oxygen helps break it down aerobically which result in hardly any Methane being produced.
6. c. 8.6 million tonnes, half of this amount was recycled in UK paper mills, the other half was sold to overseas buyers for recycling.
7. Bicycle with wheels rimmed with Iron invented in 1839 by Brit Kirkpatrick Macmillan. An earlier bike made of wood was invented in France in 1818 by Baron Karl de Drais de Sauerbrun.

8. c. 33%

General Quiz 5

1. Tendrils
2. Kept in the soil until required. They do not store well out of the ground.
3. Fruit. Used to make preserves.
4. Blackcurrants & Gooseberries
5. Western Red Cedar
6. They can tolerate cooler growing conditions
7. b. They do not freeze well. They can be stored in the freezer without problems.
8. Seeds
9. Aerating lawns
10. Oxygen levels
11. Trees
12. Aquatic plants, they let water in through the sides.
13. Bulbs are still in leaf, which helps them become established. Christmas Quiz
14. Climb without the need of support such as trellis panels.
15. Trim the hedge top to a point, like a sloping roof to prevent snow from settling.

Christmas Quiz

1. South Africa
2. Mistletoe
3. Cairngorms, Scottish Highlands
4. Holly
5. Help from Britain during WW2
6. The Star of Bethlehem
7. Cloves

8. Birch
9. One single snowflake within the 24 hour period
10. Windsor
11. Australia
12. Turkey
13. Apple Juice
14. d
15. The Nightingale
16. Dates
17. Nordmann Fir
18. Pansies
19. Ice rink
20. Brussel Sprouts

Printed in Great Britain
by Amazon.co.uk, Ltd.,
Marston Gate.